Pebble®

Great African-Americans

Bessie
COLEMAN

by Riley Flynn   Consulting Editor: Gail Saunders-Smith, PhD

CAPSTONE PRESS
a capstone imprint

Pebble Books are published by Capstone Press,
1710 Roe Crest Drive, North Mankato, Minnesota 56003
www.capstonepub.com

Library of Congress Cataloging-in-Publication Data
Flynn, Riley.
  Bessie Coleman / by Riley Flynn.
     pages cm—(Pebble books. Great African-Americans)
Audience: Ages 6-8. Audience: Grades K to 3.
Summary: "Simple text and photographs present the life of aviator Bessie Coleman"—
Provided by publisher.
Includes bibliographical references and index.
ISBN 978-1-4765-3955-3 (library binding)
ISBN 978-1-4765-5159-3 (paberpack)
ISBN 978-1-4765-6016-8 (ebook pdf)
1. Coleman, Bessie, 1896–1926—Juvenile literature. 2. African American women air
pilots—Biography—Juvenile literature. 3. Air pilots–United States–Biography—Juvenile
literature. I. Title.
TL540.C546F58 2014
629.13092—dc23 [B]   2013035322

Editorial Credits
Erika L. Shores, editor; Ashlee Suker, designer; Wanda Winch, media researcher;
Laura Manthe, production specialist

Photo Credits
Alamy: SDSAM, 12; Corbis: Underwood & Underwood, 4, 14; General Research &
Reference Division, Schomburg Center for Research in Black Culture, The New York Public
Library, Astor, Lenox and Tilden Foundations, 16, 20; Getty Images Inc: Michael Ochs
Archives, 10; Library of Congress: Prints and Photographs Division, 6; National Air and
Space Museum Archives, Smithsonian Institute, 18; Shutterstock: Vibrant Image Studio,
clouds design; Smithsonian Institution, cover, 8

Note to Parents and Teachers

The Great African-Americans set supports national curriculum standards for
social studies related to people, places, and environments. This book describes and
illustrates Bessie Coleman. The images support early readers in understanding the
text. The repetition of words and phrases helps early readers learn new words. This
book also introduces early readers to subject-specific vocabulary words, which are
defined in the Glossary section. Early readers may need assistance to read some
words and to use the Table of Contents, Glossary, Read More, Internet Sites, and
Index sections of the book.

Printed in the United States of America in North Mankato, Minnesota.
092013   007764CGS14

Table of Contents

4

Meet Bessie

Bessie Coleman was a famous pilot. She was the first African-American woman to earn a pilot's license. Bessie worked hard to make her dreams come true.

Women picking cotton around 1920

1892

born in Texas

Young Bessie

Bessie was born in Texas in 1892. Her family was poor. Bessie started working when she was very young. She picked cotton and washed clothes. Bessie wanted a more exciting life.

1892
born in Texas

1910
travels to Oklahoma
for college

Bessie and her mother worked to save money. They wanted Bessie to get an education. In 1910 Bessie went to a college in Oklahoma. She read about pilots and airplanes.
She became interested in flying.

1892
born in Texas

1910
travels to Oklahoma
for college

1920
goes to France
for flight school

As an Adult

Flight schools in the United States wouldn't teach an African-American woman. Bessie did not give up.

She learned to speak French.

In 1920 she found a flight school in France that would teach her.

1892
born in Texas

1910
travels to Oklahoma
for college

1920
goes to France
for flight school

Bessie earned her pilot's license in 1921. She became the first African-American woman to do so. When Bessie went back to the United States, she was famous. Even though she was famous, Bessie could not find a job.

1921

earns a pilot's license

1892 · born in Texas

1910 · travels to Oklahoma for college

1920 · goes to France for flight school

Bessie wanted to open a flight school for African-Americans. But she needed money. She decided she would learn to be a stunt pilot.

1921

earns a pilot's license

1892
born in Texas

1910
travels to Oklahoma
for college

1920
goes to France
for flight school

Later Years

Bessie went back to France for three months. She studied how to be a stunt pilot. She started performing stunts in 1922. Bessie began earning money to open a flight school.

1921
earns a pilot's license

1922
starts performing stunts

1892	1910	1920
born in Texas	travels to Oklahoma for college	goes to France for flight school

18

Sadly Bessie was never able to open her school. She died in 1926 after falling out of her plane. Then, in 1929, a flight school opened for African-Americans in California. The school was named after Bessie.

1921
earns a pilot's license

1922
starts performing stunts

1926
dies at age 34

Yours truly
Bessie Coleman

1892

born in Texas

1910

travels to Oklahoma
for college

1920

goes to France
for flight school

Bessie worked hard to become the first African-American woman pilot. The way Bessie followed her dreams still inspires people today.

1921
earns a pilot's license

1922
starts performing stunts

1926
dies at age 34

Glossary

college—a school students attend after high school

education—dealing with teaching and learning in school

inspire—to influence or encourage other people in a good way

pilot—a person who flies airplanes

pilot's license—a document that gives someone permission to fly an airplane

stunt—a difficult trick

Read More

Brown, Tami Lewis. *Soar, Elinor!* New York: Farrar Straus Giroux, 2010.

Rustad, Martha E. H. *Airplanes.* Smithsonian Little Explorer. North Mankato, Minn.: Capstone Press, 2014.

Wearing, Judy. *Amelia Earhart.* My Life. New York: Weigl Publishers, 2011.

Internet Sites

FactHound offers a safe, fun way to find Internet sites related to this book. All of the sites on FactHound have been researched by our staff.

Here's all you do:
Visit *www.facthound.com*
Type in this code: 9781476539553

Critical Thinking Using the Common Core

1. Bessie showed African-Americans and women that they could go to school and become pilots. Why was this considered so difficult at the time? (Key Ideas and Details)

2. Bessie wanted to do something exciting with her life, so she chose to become a pilot. What steps did she take to achieve her goal? Look at the timeline and text to answer. (Craft and Structure)

Index

Word Count: 274
Grade: 1
Early-Intervention Level: 21